DISCARDED

Elk

By JoAnn Early Macken

Reading Consultant: Jeanne Clidas, Ph.D.
Director, Roberts Wesleyan College Literacy Clinic

WEEKLY READER®
PUBLISHING

Please visit our web site at **www.garethstevens.com**.
For a free catalog describing our list of high-quality books,
call 1-877-542-2595 (USA) or 1-800-387-3178 (Canada).
Our fax: 1-877-542-2596

Library of Congress Cataloging-in-Publication Data

Macken, JoAnn Early, 1953–
    Elk / by JoAnn Early Macken. — [Rev. ed.]
        p. cm. — (Animals that live in the mountains)
    Includes bibliographical references and index.
    ISBN-10: 1-4339-2412-9   ISBN-13: 978-1-4339-2412-5 (lib. bdg.)
    ISBN-10: 1-4339-2495-1   ISBN-13: 978-1-4339-2495-8 (soft cover)
    1. Elk—Juvenile literature. I. Title.
    QL737.U55M253   2009
    599.65'42–dc22   2009000103

This edition first published in 2010 by
Weekly Reader® Books
An Imprint of Gareth Stevens Publishing
1 Reader's Digest Road
Pleasantville, NY 10570-7000 USA

Copyright © 2010 by Gareth Stevens, Inc.

Executive Managing Editor: Lisa M. Herrington
Senior Editor: Barbara Bakowski
Project Management: Spooky Cheetah Press
Cover Designers: Jennifer Ryder-Talbot and Studio Montage
Production: Studio Montage
Library Consultant: Carl Harvey, Library Media Specialist, Noblesville, Indiana

Photo credits: Cover, pp. 1, 11 Shutterstock; pp. 5, 7, 9, 19 © Tom and Pat Leeson; pp. 13, 17, 21
© Michael H. Francis; p. 15 © Jeff Milton/Daybreak Imagery

Printed in the United States of America

1 2 3 4 5 6 7 8 9 14 13 12 11 10 09

Table of Contents

Boldface words appear in the glossary.

An Elk Family

A baby elk is a **calf**. A calf has white spots on its coat. The spots make the calf hard to see.

calf

Calves drink milk from their mothers. A female elk is called a **cow**. In about a week, the calves can run. A few weeks later, they start to eat grass.

A male elk is called a **bull**.
Elk are larger than deer.
They are smaller than
moose. Like deer and
moose, elk have **hooves**
on their feet.

hooves

Life in a Herd

Elk stay in a group called a **herd**. An older cow leads a herd. One elk watches for danger.

herd

Elk use their noses, ears, and eyes to sense danger. They see things that move. They watch out for bears and cougars.

Elk eat grass and other plants. They swallow their food quickly. Later, they bring it up and chew it again.

Changing With the Seasons

Bulls have **antlers**. The antlers fall off each winter. In spring, new antlers grow.

antlers

In spring, elk move up the mountain. They look for fresh grass to eat. In fall, they move down to warmer places.

In winter, elk grow thick coats to keep warm. They dig through snow to find food. They may eat bark and twigs. In spring, they **molt**, or shed their thick coats.

Fast Facts

Height	about 5 feet (2 meters) at the shoulder
Length	about 8 feet (3 meters) nose to tail
Weight	Males: about 700 pounds (318 kilograms) Females: about 500 pounds (227 kilograms)
Diet	grasses, shrubs, tree bark, and twigs
Average life span	up to 12 years

Glossary

antlers: the branched horns of animals in the deer family

bull: a male elk

calf: a baby elk

cow: a female elk

herd: a large group of elk or other animals

hooves: hard coverings on animals' feet

molt: to shed hair, skin, horn, or feathers

For More Information

Books

Bugling Elk and Sleeping Grizzlies: The Who, What, and When of Yellowstone and Grand Teton National Parks. Shirley A. Craighead (Falcon, 2004)

Elk. Northern Trek (series). Scott Wrobel (Smart Apple Media, 2004)

Web Sites

Elk
animals.nationalgeographic.com/animals/mammals/elk.html
Watch a video of elk making their "bugling" call.

Elk
www.eparks.org/wildlife_protection/wildlife_facts/elk.asp
Find out where you can see elk in the wild.

Index

About the Author

JoAnn Early Macken is the author of two rhyming picture books, *Sing-Along Song* and *Cats on Judy*, and more than 80 nonfiction books for children. Her poems have appeared in several children's magazines. She lives in Wisconsin with her husband and their two sons.